Twenty-Five Reasons to Vote For Republicans

by

Anthony Rutledge, Ph.D.

Twenty-Five Reasons
To Vote for Republicans

by

Anthony Rutledge, Ph.D.
Professor Emeritus – Political Science

ISBN-10: 1544621507

ISBN-13: 978-1544621500

TABLE OF CONTENTS

CHAPTER 1

ELIMINATING CORPORATE INFLUENCE IN GOVERNMENT

CHAPTER 2

ELIMINATING TAX LOOPHOLES FOR MILLIONAIRES

CHAPTER 3

ELIMINATING CORPORATE WELFARE

CHAPTER 4

SUPPORT FOR ORGANIZED LABOR

CHAPTER 5

SUPPORT FOR A LIVING MINIMUM WAGE

CHAPTER 6

SUIPPORTING GENDER EQUALITY

CHAPTER 7

PUBLIC SUPPORT FOR THE ARTS

CHAPTER 8

SUPPORT FOR PUBLIC EDUCATION

CHAPTER 9

PROMOTING SOCIAL EQUALITY

CHAPTER 10

ENHANCING SOCIAL PROGRAMS FOR THE POOR

CHAPTER 11

SUPPORTING VOTING RIGHTS
FOR MINORITIES

CHAPTER 12

SUPPORTING LGBTQ RIGHTS

CHAPTER 13

SUPPORTING A WOMAN'S
RIGHT TO CHOOSE

CHAPTER 14

SUPPORTING EMBRYONIC STEM CELL RESEARCH

CHAPTER 15

EXPANDING AND ENHANCING MEDICAID AND MEDICARE

CHAPTER 16

DECREASING GUN VIOLENCE -
CLOSING LOOPHOLES

CHAPTER 17

EQITABLE SENTENCING FOR DRUG OFFENDERS

CHAPTER 18

ELIMINATING THE DEATH PENALTY

CHAPTER 19

REFORMING SENTENCING FOR NON-VIOLENT CRIMES

CHAPTER 20

PROTECTING CLEAN AIR AND WATER

CHAPTER 21

PROTECTING FORESTS AND WETLANDS

CHAPTER 22

PROTECTING ENDANGERED SPECIES

CHAPTER 23

ELIMINATING FOSSIL FUELS

CHAPTER 24

SUPPORTING CLEAN ENERGY

CHAPTER 25

REVERSING GLOBAL WARMING

DISCLAIMER

Any resemblance to persons named in this work, including the author, whether living or dead, is purely coincidental. Periodicals cited on the back cover are purely fictional. This work is intended to be an entertaining way for Democrats to look at Republicans through the lens of Democrat Party positions on major issues. The issues are serious, the presentation is frivolous. Please enjoy your time with this book.

- Anthony Rutledge, Ph.D. Author

www.ingramcontent.com/pod-product-compliance
Lightning Source LLC
Chambersburg PA
CBHW062142280526
45788CB00001B/275